à
la
carte
my
heart

by

James Hickey

sunshine press

À la Carte My Heart by James Hickey
ISBN 978-0-992-5421-1-5
Copyright © James Hickey. All rights reserved.
First Published 2015 by Sunshine Press
Cover Design and other artwork by James Hickey
Publication Production Services by Connie M. Berg
Photography by Marjorie Rose

A heart can't break if it's soaked in wine,
It just gets pushed around from time to time.

Life

Sleep's Embrace 1
Plastic Fruit 3
Progress? 5
Smart Phonobia 7
Soft Edges 9
1976 11
Why Whale? 13
Reconnaissance of Self 15
Mind the Gap 18
Day in the Life of a Mole 19
The Forgotten Ones 20
Life on a Cigarette Paper 21
Generation Gap 22
While it is Still Dark 23
Evolution of Desire 25
How Long is a Piece of Boring? 28
Ode to Coffee 29
The Day the Night Slept 31

Love

What the Heart Does	35
Tough Love Lady Luck	36
Acrobatic Heart	37
What is the Up?	38
The Raven's Cry	39
This Place is Familiar	40
Your Jacket Nearly Stayed	41
Much too Much	42
Thoughtful Love	44
What Has Transpired?	45
Sweet Inebriated Requietedness	46
Is this as Close as I Get?	47
Where the Lines End	49
Random Objects of Affection	51
Call and Response	52
The Walking Cane	53
Awkwardness in the Room	55

Part 1:

Life

Sleep's Embrace
6.11.2012

Sleep is my escape so I entice it.
I draw its velvet blanket over me
Until it has enveloped myself.
Nothing can pierce or penetrate this surrender.
Like an island out at sea
Sleep keeps away all the troubles that haunt me.

Sleep's touch is warm like a lover's.
Like a lover it draws me in deep
And soothes my incompleteness
Until my exhaustion is spent.
It calls to me when I try to hide
And hides me when others try to call.
Sleep berates weariness until the scourge does repent.

I am devoted to sleep paying homage nightly
And in the afternoon if I am feeling unsprightly.
Sleep's shrine occupies spaces sacred and not -
Like the honeymoon suite and the park bench,
The abbey's cloists and the sailor's wench,
The princes' chair and the digger's trench.

Sleep stands on a train, huddles in rain
Captures others at the wheel.
It is the iceberg that convinces steel
To relinquish its strength
And allow the stricken vessel
To plunge to the ocean's depths.

It flirts with death in a winter's frost,
Softens the blow of summer's midday fist,
Jousts with illness while the body rests,
And causes pain itself to desist.

No greater ally have I than this,
But to close my eyes and be at peace.

Plastic Fruit
28.7.2013

Plastic hangs in the trees like fruit.

It is the kind grown in the fertilised soil of unethical consumption,
Mulched by the plastic generation.

But who will harvest this fruit?
The future people who will learn how to eat it?
The next-gen birds whose metabolism will cater
For the gut-strangling strands of indigestible poly-carbons?
Those fish who will evolve the ability to convert take-away coffee lids
Into scales of immortality,
Only killed when they are caught by bears with a taste
For anything from a two dollar shop.

And the fake plastic fruit on the kitchen table
Will be consumed by school kids who are able
To bite into the mal-nutritious doppelgangers.

And the dog won't bring the ball back unless it's organic,
Because the poly-vinyl acetate
Will make the K-9 salivate
Causing it to masticate
Every last Spalding-ace.

The cat will feast on plastic toy mice and milk bottles diced
Into sardine-sized morsels
And plastic milk bottle-lid droppings
Will lie beneath kitti-litter scrapings.

And those cows where the plastic milk bottles come from
Will chew their cud on astro-turf
And their four-chambered stomachs
Will form the production line
For all the single-use forks and knives
Required by this take away life.

The plastic clouds will send down a cacophony
Of every once-off object we will ever need
We will replace the sun with a disco ball
Which we will throw away when the batteries run low
For no one will know
How to think anymore
For our brains will have become
Solid...resin...globules...housing...a single...plastic...gold fish
That never learns from its mistakes.

And the plastic fruit will hang on the dead tree's bow
Until it slowly, slowly breaks.

Progress?
20.2.2013

Blind escarpments loom with houses for blinkers
    They no longer see the valley below
    Like horses poised for a gallop
    At gates forever closed

Yet progress races down to the trees
    Lingers at the edge of urban growth,
    Until demand makes it pause
    Then sprawl can take a breath

So the dozer and chainsaw exhale
    The developer's dossier stills,
    Then greed says 'Look here,
    There's probably gold in these hills'.

So in an eye's blink there are terraces cut
    The outcrop converted to crown
    And the place they call Broken Hill
    Has a ruby like this next to town.

But not just here can this work be seen
    There's a story like this everywhere,
    And former people never see a cent
    Trees vanish into air.

So mind your step when you walk the streets
    Take care where your foot does tread,
    These paved and walled objects
    Are built on the lives of the dead.

Build your house, build it well
    Call it your place, your soul,
    Do not be surprised when they knock at your door
    And geld you like a foal.

Finally you will understand
    The people who sleep out of doors,
    Who don't drink to get drunk
    But to forget what the rest ignore.

For once was owned by someone else
    That patch of dirt you bought,
    It will be swept from beneath your feet
    In the saddle of progress we are caught.

Smart Phonobia
4.5.2013

What is this thing in my pocket?
      It has no buttons.
      It is not a flip phone.

It's as strange as a bar where I've never been,
So when I walk in everyone looks at me,
Like I have no right to be there,
Despite my name being carved on the wall
Of the lady's toilets in gross obscenities.

I haven't been here before,
      Owning a phone
      Without buttons.

Where people are trapped inside
This thin gold-fish bowl social aquarium that travels with,
That lets you pull and push,
And ignore people as if,
They were apparitions,
While you point to with your index
At those trapped in the electro-teledex .

I carry a stranger in my pocket.
      Without buttons,
      It is not a flip phone.

It is not a flip phone, it's a phoney, a mirage,
Not really my friend though it holds all of them,
There they are behind glass, away from my grasp.

So turn it off and enjoy the day,
The pub, the people, the oxygen, the smoke,
The inhalation of the immediate that drips from every
Wall, chair, object,
Laugh, cry, shout and blaspheme
Against the strangers we now carry,
Like a thief carries a sack of pilferings,
Except the smart phone is the bandit and we are the bounty.

It is not a flip phone in my pocket,
    And no,
        I am not happy to tag you.

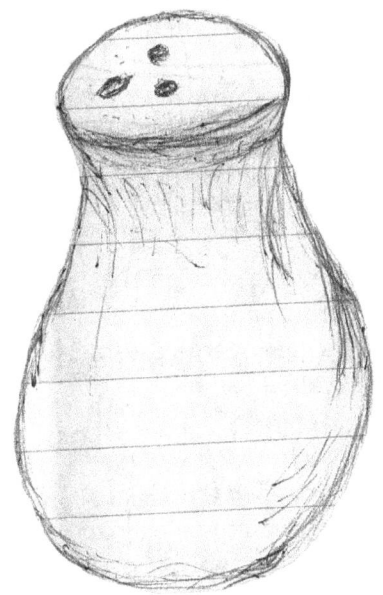

Soft Edges
14.2.2013

There are soft edges on the highway
There is barrenness beyond
There's a haze that lingers when you drive in a way
        That leaves the sun behind

There are footprints in the headlights
There are creatures living out here
There's dust in my hair and it's been there for days
        That keeps me and bush in twine.

There are troubles in this country
There's rain that runs off their backs
There's politik thick as a flooded river plain
        That sweetens no track of mine!

There is you downstream south a-ways
There's a stretch of road between
There's a banged-up wagon that might get me home
        That keeps me alert of mind

There are fallen fences and piles of steel
There are eagles soaring past
There's a drover watching over saltbush plains
        That cattle walk single-file

There's wildlife strewn both left and right
There are ravens having their fill
There's a sign that begs you to take a nap
        That might just keep you alive

There are tracks that turn like us to dust
There are ashes sprinkled on the verge
There's a forest that died a long time ago
      That stands in slow decline

There are trees that read 'Jesus return is near'
There's a good chance the good Lord forgot
There are souls few and far on the Australian bush track
      That to find them would take a divine.

1976
16.8.2013

Do you miss 1976?
When your beard was black
And all your friends were young?
At that Christmas party where you liked Julie
And she liked him,
But it didn't matter in 1976.

Would you go back to that Christmas in 1976,
Before your friends had families and
You'd take that chance to give her a kiss
Because by next Christmas she'd be married to someone else?
And that picture on the wall would tell the story over and over.

Would you if you could go back to '76
And tell all those people
To never forget this Christmas?
How much of that night shaped your life?
And where were the limits?

And you do go back to 1976
Every time you look at that picture
And just wait for that night to return
And it does,
And you're back,
You're back to that Christmas drinks in 1976.

1976   16/8/13
1976

Do you miss 1976
When your beard was black
And all your friends were young at that Christmas party. Where you liked Julie and she liked him but it didn't matter in 1976. Would you go back to when your beard was black to that Christmas in 1976 before your friends had families and you never even knew it would be something to miss, and you'd take that chance to give her a kiss because by next Christmas she'd be married to someone else, and that picture on the wall would tell the story over and over. Would you go back to 1976 if you could and tell all those people you loved just then to never forget this Christmas in 1976. How much of that night stayed your life, and the limits were no where to be seen and you do go back to 1976 everytime you look at that picture hanging and just waite for that moment to return and it does, and you're back, you're back to that Christmas drinks in 1976

Why Whale?
Based on a dream
5.12.2012

I met a whale in my sleep last night
        He was stuck on a riverbank
I told him I was stuck in love
        To this his heart sank

We exchanged our names I told him mine
        He looked me in the eyes
Then he spoke his as a long breath of wind
        Which soothed me to the bones

That name was full of many things
        A long life of joy and sorrow
Yet in this state so desperate
        His voice bore the scent of peace

He cared not for his own dilemma
        Precarious beyond compare
He asked whose harpoon has wounded
        Surely love brings not despair?

I said love is a violent arrow
        I care for its injury no more
I would take it and arrest it
        Then dash it to the ocean's floor

Stay you, he said, stay you a while
        If the harpoon has no line
Then bathe in the waters of our fair lady's sea
        The salt will dissolve it in time

I knew he was right and with his last
        He had awakened hope where none was
He spoke to my life and cared not for his
        I would like to own a heart like this

So I took his words and made them fruitful
        I swam the ocean deep and wide
I learnt the things that he had known
        And let life ebb with the tide

That whale's bones still stand in the mud
        Proud and tall as in life
His name when I speak it to strangers exclaim:
'What a friend, what a friend, what a friend!'

Reconnaissance of Self
6.11.2013

To be alone is to be one.
>All of me and none of anyone else.
>To spend time not sharing,
>So when the search is over
>I will be reconciled to myself.

The rehab starts with anonymity.
>No one else can find me -
>Only I know where I am hid.
>Where under a rock I crawled
>Waiting for my chrysalis.

When I was older and the voices said,
>You'll be no good, you'll be no good.
>Before my voice fell,
>Like an auctioneer's late hammer:

>>My peel I let them zest,
>>My zeal they did arrest,
>>Did feel it on my breast,
>>Their seal of un-interest,
>>Each meal of jest did my soul digest.

Then later did they govern still
>What was left of me until,
>I walked as a ghost,
>Through each moment lost,
>A cup that will not fill.

So I'll search the corner of every room,
> Behind each barren tree,
> Under any object
> That will let me beneath.
> I'll uncover the places where I hide
> And share with you this remaining life.

19/10/13

Mind the step behind you as you leave, mind it doesn't follow you, keep moving from those things that stop you, and steps that follow you thi like a ghost, follow no ones steps but your own, breathe new air each day, bathe in fresh sunshine that has yet to be reflected, be the object that shines on others, so they too can see the steps they must avoid and the path that is theirs to journey, and began your own every moment of this short, brilliant existence. !

Day in the Life of a Mole
18.5.2013

Darkness, darkness
        Dig, dig
Silence, silence
        Dig, dig
What do you expect when you live underground?
A life lived in darkness without a sound

Dirt and dampness
        Worms and rats
That's the company with whom you'll sleep
Under the earth that's the company you'll keep

Gold and diamonds
        Rubies and Jade
Are worth no pearls beneath earth's shade
In days of hunger they'll prove no aid.

You are rich, you are poor,
        You are blind and deaf
Inconsequential in the life of a mole
The only thing to measure is the depth of the soul.

The Forgotten Ones
3.6.2012

There they sit waiting for news
        No one will visit, it's just not done
You won't survive on the air you breathe
        It's too thin for you to sustain

There not even birds will fly
        It is easy to see why
The forgotten ones are filed away
        From warmth of any kind

There I would if I could go
        To say this is not the end
Here is a note to help days pass
        In time we will laugh my friend

There you are my lonesome brother
        You've found yourself at last
You are not forgotten anymore
        The stolen time has past.

Life on a Cigarette Paper
16.2.2012

Framed by four edges

Folded in the middle

Rolled up tight

Set alight

Sucked

Stubbed

Regret

Relit

Salvaged

Savoured

Start again

Right the wrongs

Forget all that has past

Figure out new ways.

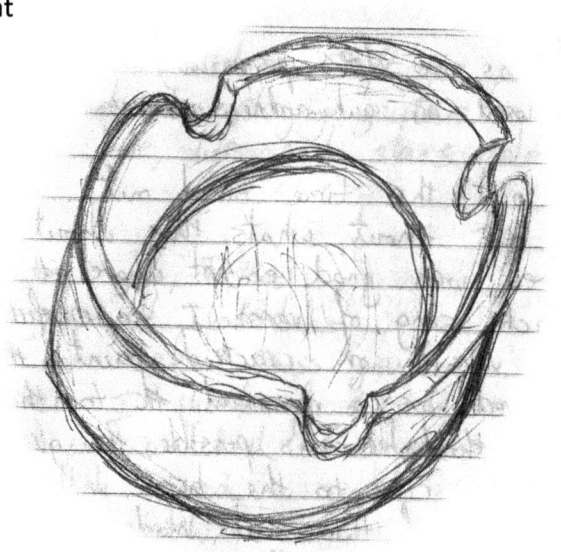

Generation Gap
3.6.2012

You say 'like',
      I say 'for example'
You say 'lets skype',
      I say 'I'm not able'
You send texts while walking down the street
I thought an apple is something you eat

I say 'one meg',
      You say 'terabyte'
I say 'I agree',
      You say 'yeah, I know right'
You tag people in every photo that you take
I remember when corn was the only flake

You say 'Spotify',
      I say 'CD',
You say 'bit torrent',
      I say 'VideoEzy',
You've never heard of the A-Team or M*A*S*H
I've never used the tag of hash

I say 'coffee?',
      You say 'energy'
I say 'lets hang',
      You say 'chat with me'
So many ways to contact each other
If it doesn't work out I could always try your mother.

While it is Still Dark
4.7.2011

The stranger and I sit down to breakfast
  While it is still dark.
I sip my tea and think of the day ahead
  While she continues to feast.
Where my sustenance is processed grain
  Hers is processed wood.
I am reminded she is there with each click of her teeth
  Like some out of time clock.

I am not alone as the others sleep
  While it is still dark.
For you are here.
I thought I rose early to work
  Yet here you are toiling away
  Before the sun has met the day.
So my mind is bent
  On the actions that must be took
With hook and line and every other crook
  Written in death's book.

What task have you set yourself to
  While it is still dark?
Carving a labyrinth behind the cupboard?
  A tunnel to the rice, a gap to reach the honey?
A cavern in the wall to store the wares
  Which you have mischieviously and deviously acquired?

You will meet your end
  While it is still dark,
When I this trap have set,
 And your last meal will be like my breath,
  Held and baited.
Industrious little fucker though you may be,
You are here with me
  While it is still dark.

The Evolution of Desire
19.3.2014

Ego one
Bird, go away from me, it is not my job to feed. You have a sore foot? It is no concern of mine. You can find my scraps when I am done but I will not toss you even a crumb. Don't bother me for I have more important things on my mind than your one-eyed stare. Your hunger is of no consequence and whether you live or die brings neither joy nor grief, celebration or relief, and does not add to my belief that your life is worth no more than that fallen leaf.

Ego two
Dear God, help me, I am in need, I am hungry, please feed all my wildest desires and take pity on my brokenness. You see, I come to you and beg on one knee and ask for sympathy. You hold all things in one palm and you could scatter a few grains in my furrowed field. I haven't eaten in a week, I can barely sleep, all my dreams are haunted by death as it comes for my soul to reap. I don't ask for pity just one seed that I can nurture and never bother you again, Dear God Please!!!

Ego one
Bird, why are you still here? You have wings, find a field full of the fruits of your diet. This city is no place for you, among us superior beings. This is a city not a place for your feathers to preen. We have commerce and conversations, not worms and brooding places. If I give you a speck of food will you go away? No, you will call to your friends and they too will make of my lunch their demands. No. I will sit as I please with my bread and my cheese and you can search for a skerrick of life as I leave.

Ego two
Dear God, I am hung over today. Take my pain away, this to thee I pray. So much consumption I have never had, nor will I again I swear it on my own head. Oh, the throbbing, the eyes that despise their appointed task, the nose that smells all too well the mixture of beer and wine, vomit and pills. The tastebuds on my tongue searching a dry mouth, for a liquid that last night led it east and west, north and south. A skin that feels like it was left on the sidewalk, and crawled home and is now outlined with white chalk. And ears, wretched ears will you stop at nothing, in convincing me there is a fire in every corner of this shell of a building called self. God my spirit is willing but my flesh is like peat, used to make a whisky of weakness taken neat.

Ego one
Flap your wings, bird! Perch on someone else's pity. I have none for you, feathered shrew.

Ego two
Give my desires flight, dear God. Elevate me and set me apart.

Ego one
Be-gone seagull, dwarfed pelican, duck-footed pigeon, homeless sparrow!

Ego two
Shelter and warmth, love and affection, a feather pillow to rest my head.

Ego one
Your neck! I could break it.

Ego two
Preserve me Lord.

Ego one
Squawk!

Ego two
Squawk?

Ego one & Ego Two
Squawk! Squawk! Squawk!

How Long is a Piece of Boring?
2.12.2013

I'm bored of the conversations I hear,
Bored of the places I drink,
Bored of this lunch break,
Bored of tattoos,
Bored of no tattoos,
Bored of moustaches,
Bored of air conditioning, alley ways,
      sun glasses, subways
      moving, staying,
      sharing, not caring,
Public displays of affection,
Private museums of inaffection,
Death and resurrection and this life unlasting,
Bored of time wasted on things I won't be remembered for,
And bored of remembering people
Who must have been bored when they met me
Because they have no idea who I am.

Bored of my own existence.

I'm not bored of the ocean so thank Christ for that.
Hopefully one of the above isn't bored of me yet.

Ode to Coffee
20.3.2014

I drink coffee
>Because I am bored at work,
>Because I am lonely,
>Because I like the smell more than the taste,
>Because tea reminds me of my childhood
>And coffee is an adult drink.

I drink coffee
>Because I can't drink hard liquor at work,
>Even though it would be better than the hit of
>Pseudo adrenalin.

I drink coffee
>Because it hasn't rained for a while,
>Because it has been raining too long,
>Because your face might appear through the crowd,
>Because Saturday mornings were never that bad,
>Just the Friday nights I couldn't stand.

I drink coffee
>To be seen drinking coffee while
>Reading an important piece of literature.
>Because I no longer care for horticulture
>And I don't know where the beans came from,
>Be it a cat, ferret,
>Or some disgruntled Holden employee.

I drink coffee
>Because I can't stand drinking from a can,
>Because QANTAS used to say I can,
>Because Malaysian Airlines don't give a damn.

I drink coffee
    Because it is and isn't in fashion,
    Because I have no reason,
    In any economic first home owners grant
    Get it before end of financial year season.

I drink coffee
    To lose an hour,
    Because you have no idea where I've been
        in the last 24 hours,
    Not buying someone else flowers,
    Just existing inside myself,
    Breathing in my own caffeine
    And sipping myself slowly into oblivion.

You want to know why I drink coffee?
Next time I ask just come join me.

The Day the Night Slept
20.7.2013

I wonder how you manage
When you play in high heels.
Seems to defy reality
But you do so well,
And you play so soft.
I wonder are you the same in life.
Your deep eyes weighed down
By eye lashes that fight the day's end,
    Daring it to make you stop.

For just when the night was supposed
To check if we were asleep,
It heard your song and slept a moment,
And in that blink you stole the keys to every lullaby,
And unlocked everyone's dreams
So they danced in every corner of the world,
And no one knew why they were happy.
The night had no power,
    Against your songs in that hour.

The keys for the locks you flung into the sea,
So each dream could never again be shut away,
And now the night is just a moment,
And those dreams are a way of life,
Not stowed away in the dark parts of us,
We will live them until,
We forget how to wake,
And thus sleep,
Dreaming of those we lived,
    When we had the chance.

So sing without reserve
In knowledge it will move even the night,
To admit it once dreamed of being,
And in dreaming it was no longer one moment,
But a part of every moment,
That ever was or will be.
And finally dear muse,
May your heavy eye lashes
Grant you rest,
      For daylight has arrived at last.

Part 2:

Love

What the Heart Does
3.10.13

The heart longs for creatures
       it can never hold

The heart hopes for those
       it will never know

The heart believes it knows
       the love it needs
And grieves as it breaks
       for those it did forsake

The heart twists and bends
       as old wounds try to mend

And blooms again
       when it finally finds a friend

The heart longs
       but to fate it does belong.

Tough Love Lady Luck
2.8.2012

I am not in love with you.

I was in love with the idea of being in love.
>But now I've found someone else
To be in love with the idea of
>Being in love with.

I like that idea,
>I like it a lot.
So much more appealing
>Than its practical application
So I'm drifting from one love to the next
>But never getting my anchor wet.

I could love you, that is a great idea!
>But you are busy and your life is drear.
My life is great but I can't get laid.
>When I try I end up falling in love.
If I aim for love I still don't get laid.

Lady you're out there and you are in luck
>Because I'm in love.

Not with you, yet,
But you'll be next, I bet.
Then your sister, and mother,
>Maybe even your brother.

Who knows where it'll end.
>Probably as friends.
And I'll tell myself the love I felt
>Was just pretend.

Acrobatic Heart
21.10.2013

Your heart is a circus,
      Performing acrobatic tricks,
Leaping through love's fire,
      Like costumed pigs.
One after the other,
      A ludicrous display,
Not a pleasant sight,
      Hearts burnt this way.
High above the ring,
      Other lovers move with ease,
They hold each other firmly,
      Swinging on their trapeze.
While on the ground you hover,
      You catch whoever falls,
But the tumbling ones are broken,
      Their hearts have many walls.
A circus moves around,
      When it has run its course,
But your tent pegs plunge deep,
      You know just one discourse.
Clowns that juggle, dogs that talk,
      Elephants dressed in drag,
All balanced on a single beam,
      That tends to bend and sag.
Acrobatic heart that is full of doubt,
      And full of nothing else,
Fill yourself with sterner stuff,
      Or just amuse yourself.

What is the up?
25.1.2013

A zip that goes to nowhere
A kiss that was left un-dared
Your hips you kept quite un-bared
      For me that sums it up

A thought for you left unwed
I fought to have you in bed
I taught you all that my head
      Had brewed to fill your cup

My brow has kept its furrow
From now since I in sorrow
Gave bow to stages morrow
      No audience will erupt

You are what I in retro
In part I meant to love-throw
My heart was never to know
      You offered none to sup

Forget those times left facing
Of set, game, match straight acing
I bet I'll soon be racing
      To sign another pre-nup.

The Raven's Cry
13.12.2012

I sit and let my thoughts drift.
        I sit and sip and sit.
I thought they would never settle but they did
        On you one last time.
On the sheltered cove that you are no more
        No haven for my thoughts you are.

On the brink I now stand
        Looking upon unfamiliar lands
This man has seen enough to know
        He can't meet what life demands
This clouded sky my demeanor manifest
        Written in the heavens my tempered unrest
No more tests can I forthwith endure
        Blue horizon please knock at my door.

The raven cries for the evening star
        To the raven not a cry but a laugh
To my melancholy state this bird relates
        And tempests my crest-fallen heart
Speak the truth you raving aviare!
        You bird of prey where victim is despair!
'Nevermore' says the raven but I know it is mistaken
        T'wil be back when it gets a chance.

There is no way to stop you getting to me
        I can't halt the raven in flight.
I could shoot the bird, avoid you like the plague
        But the thoughts and sentiments remain.
So fuck off bird you cunt with wings!
        Go rouse someone else's feelings.
I'm off to the pub, for a beer and a tug
        With her, or with her, or maybe even Doug.

This Place is Familiar
6.2.2010

This place is familiar but not.
It is full of things but not what we had.
It speaks of emptiness that cannot be filled.
It talks of you and wonders where you are.

    Search, search, search.

And I tell the place I sent you away
Because I needed space.
So the walls of the place move in
And the place grows angry
I miss her says the place
We bonded through child birth
Do not separate us
We are one, she is here still
Now my walls will close in like labour pains
And you will feel the miscarriage of your promises.

    Contraction, contraction, contraction.

Now I am in a room where I cannot straighten,
In this position I must remain.
I push but the place inhales with anger
Forcing my knees to my chest.
Then the place says, I thought I knew you but I do not.

    Get out, get out, get out.

You are a stranger and I will not have you here.
Find a place that will be your friend for I cannot.

Your Jacket Nearly Stayed
23.9.2013

The seat is still warm where you were sat,
    The jacket nearly left keeps your shoulders like that,

Gone long enough for shadows to creep in,
    I feel the twitch, like a light switch, like salt damp
    seeping in,

This moment under lights so dim I strain my eyes,
    With your sounds in my ears I head home by and by,

There is no exit off this path,
    The only way through is to conquer doubt,

Better off alive? Better off dead?
    Better sleeping it off instead.

Much too Much
25.9.2013

Much, too much in love
      To be any use to her

Much too full of my own thoughts
      Retreating like a cur

Much, too much absorbed in faux
      Constructing things not made

Much reality unreconciled
      In fiction do I braid

Much, too much disarmament
      Have I carried out

Much defense have I removed
      A horseless Paul Revere.

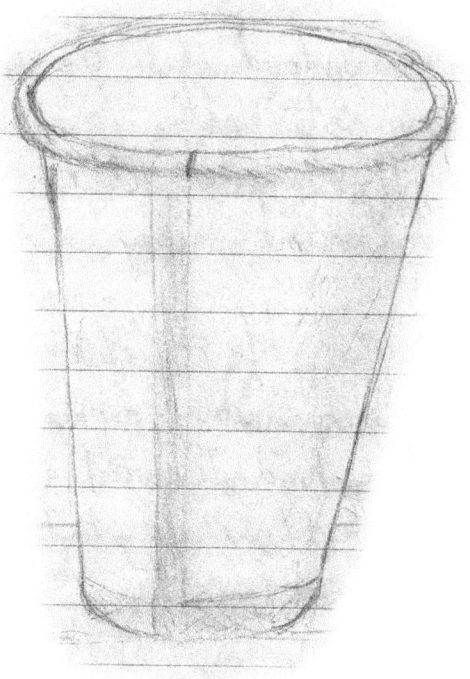

Thoughtful Love
20.9.2013

Stirred by the currents of each new love,
Drowned by the burden of a turbid mind,
Too thoughtful for love am I.

Though love will flow where it wills,
I will it to fill me 'til it spills.

I'll build a dam to catch the ebbs,
This engineered passion will bring me dregs.

Love is a hook, dangling from a cork,
Tossed by floods, grounded by drought.

I tried to follow her through the mire of doubt
But the path went in circles,
Tracking my own foot prints it turns out.

Like beast to water there's a well-worn path,
But the trail found not the affections sought.

When love wets that furrow laid down by wearied foot,
I hope each sodden step will lead me to your thoughts.

What has Transpired?
18.5.2012

Is this transition complete?
New chapter about to begin?
      At what cost?
      Is there a debt?
When will emotional foreclosure occur?
      Next week, month, year?

I expect a super crash on the
      Annuation of my youth.
How long will this system of self-reliance last?
      A week, month, year?

Am I carried by some other force?
The struggle produces what?
      A meltdown?
Emotional health about to go super-critical.
      When?
      A week, month, year?

A life-line at youth's cusp
      I've come back to where I once aimed
      The aberration was what?
      Unclear.
They are now simply
      Weeks, months and years.

Sweet Inebriated Requietedness
16.8.2013

I'm your inebriated lover
        you only kiss when you're drunk,
Well I'm halfway to being lost
        and you're halfway to kissing me.

But you won't, not until you've washed away your fears,
Those ghosts of yesterday's spirits
        that lurk in every drop
Until they drown in the fumes that rise from your insides,
        and your heart can feel again,
And for the next few hours you'll be invincible.

A heart can't break if it's soaked in wine,
It just gets pushed around from time to time.

So kiss me when you are sober
        and hold me when you are drunk,
Don't leave me stunned
        in your head-lights as you run,
Hoping if your friends don't see it,
        It won't hurt when all is said and done.

You drink to get sober and I drink to forget,
Somewhere in the middle is where we met.

Is this as Close as I get?
12.9.2013

Is this as close as I get,
Perched on a piano stool,
      Watching your fingers move.

If only they would move for me,
Play a tune on my insides,
      Feel the flats and sharps of my heart.

Sing in that key that awakens me,
From depths that can only,
      Be fathomed by a baritone.

I will not know another until I know you,
You will not love another,
      You don't want to.

Damn this poet's heart that wants to love,
But like a poem all is written,
      Before begun.

Opening verse so full of promise,
By second stanza,
      Dreaming up another.

The closing lines jumping off a bridge,
With thoughts cast over,
      The next green ridge.

Poet's heart you are a curse,
Your feeble constitution,
        Probably needed a nurse.

If hind sight were not bollocks,
I would've stuck around,
        Not left on a reflex.

So to the one I cannot forget,
Here's to being,
        As close as I get.

Where the Lines End
28.3.2013

To be two solid lines, complete and whole
That run together into the distance
      Which is the destination
Not wanting arrival but the journey.

To stop is to break and the brake was applied.
The lines ask:

      Why did we stop?
      We quelled the flow.
      We thought too much.
      We pondered and plundered
      The fruits that were ours.
      The harvest by the roadside
      Is now rotting sheaves
      Reaped and left in the autumn dampness
      The grain once so rich with promise
      Of loaves and dough,
            Pastries and brews,
            Pastas and things to start the day.
      Now the bread that begged to rise
      Is a thousand seeds un-germinated
      The pastries unrolled lie flat among weeds
      Potential brews ferment in the midday sun
      And this day will falter,
      It never even began.

So the lines that stopped are broken,
The destination reached.
Where are we?
We are not.
You are.
I am.
So it will remain.

Random Objects of Affection
3.10.2013

Tin box,
        dripping tap,
Grain of wood,
        lover's trap,
Broken arrows,
        bending winds,
Bellowing smoke,
        buckling trends,
Soon enough,
        far away,
Lost at sea,
        brand new day,
Drug of choice,
        some bad habits,
Late for lunch,
        hats and rabbits,
Caught in irons,
        crumpled jeans,
Hang me up,
        stop the crease,
Madness averted,
        not for long,
He'll be back,
        ever strong,
You're in Kansas,
        canvas tent,
This affair,
        just ain't meant.

Call and Response
By Amelie Botrill and James Hickey
22-23.9.2013

call
This grey morning I've been up since dawn
Watching blue ribbons dance
        into the cracks between clouds
When the sun split the sky I saw your face
In the shadows on a lonely wall
        that belonged somewhere in Mexico -
That place with the mustard gold windows and dark, soulful
   eyes
Perhaps it is there that I'll see you again as I did
That night that I stood in the rain
And studied your face like a Renoir girl.

response
I examined you like a Beat Poet
Face soaked in unknowns in between poems
Where your face and my inclination is apparent
Where my window frame is paned
        with no glass but this desire
To go anywhere in shade or star-shine
And the waning moon peers in through Venetian emotions
Letting you in a little and me out a bit
And this dance has me up til later than reason permits
Hope there is a reason to be up yet.

The Walking Cane
4.6.2013

I'm running with a cane in my hand.
Who cares why?
I just am.
Is it because someone is calling,
Saying they need somewhere to stay?
Saying life ain't worth living,
Saying they want to dissolve away.

I'm running with a cane in my hand.
To a place where I think there is a need.
When the other end is crying,
It is best to take heed,
Never write it off as an attention plead.

I'm running with a cane in my hand.
Most people won't understand,
Why a man who appears crippled,
Is charging down a narrow lane.
There's no one to blame,
Just a friend who tonight,
Has taken despair for a name.

So I lay this walking cane down among strangers.
You'll never believe how much they like the feel.
There's crooked lives in every bar,
Reaching out for something real,
Tangible and tactile darling,
Lean on this awhile.

I'm running with a cane in my hand.
I am your brother let me help you where I can.
This walking cane it ain't much use,
I don't need it to get around.
I just carry it incase,
someone else is on the low and down.

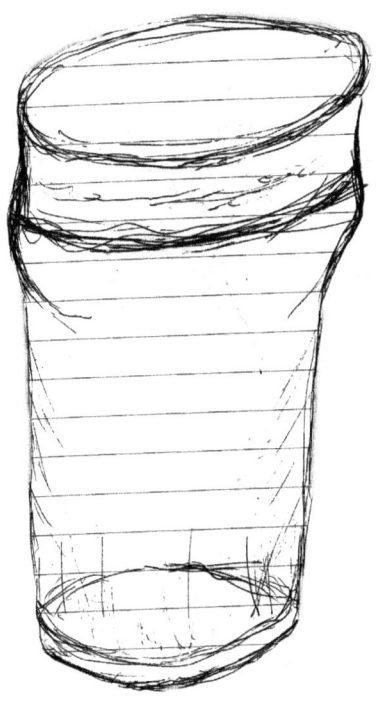

Awkwardness in the Room
4.4.2013

      I went that night to see her perform - I was the awkwardness that wouldn't leave the room.

The culmination of a summer romance
Was this night where music meant nothing
And the look of love was not in her eyes.

      The embodiment of awkwardness refuses to leave the room.

I could have met her folks that night but the coin was flipped
      And the queen's face was downcast,
Displeased with our union as her parents would have been.
We were no more,
Like a meteor burnt by the atmosphere,

      Emerging as a speck of dust,
      Trampled under-foot,
      Swept away from the door,

Where love was carried but never entered,
The threshold reached but the lovers were out of breath,
The bonds broken by a tide of sinuating circumstances,
Plotted since time began.

      And awkwardness considers leaving the room via the closest exit.

The music rings out as my internals shout,
What is this all about?
Each sculptured emotion now varnish on cracked paint,
The fissures preserved as a memorial to when

The glass was half-full and rising,
With sweet golden ale glistening,
In the glow of two souls made for each other,
But not made to make another.

I often wonder -
Does procreation make the heart grow fonder?
Or does it send our loins asunder,
And allow the sword of unrest to love's apple plunder?

    Awkwardness is hungry and is searching for an apple in a sea of oranges.

It is not enough to have love.
Battlements must be built to keep the enemy's arrows at bay,
    As they try to cut the lover's stay.
You say we have connection worth its fight,
    But with the first arrow you took flight.
As did I.
I ran like wind split at the bluff,
    A headland that told me I am not good enough.

Each passenger has a limit on the baggage they can bring,
I brought enough for four people and you had carry-on only.

Still it could have worked.
But now I retire my desire for this proverb,
And my life is no longer an adjective but a noun,
    Named goodbye.

    So awkwardness left the room that night,
    Examined love and life,
    And like each star,
    Was alone again at last.

Special thanks to:

Stuart Ready, Connie Berg, Rob Dekoch, Mike Hopkins, Mathew Drogemuller, Katerina Bryant, Ross Vosvotekas, and Amelie Botrill.

James Hickey was born and half-raised in country Queensland where cricket and bike riding were *à la mode*. He now lives in Adelaide, South Australia and has done so for most of his adult life. Music has been a constant throughout his journey, playing piano from an early age and picking up guitar a little later. Writing emerged towards the end of high school with James trying his hand as a song-smith. Poetry has only recently become a separate entity from James' song writing, manifesting in this his first publication. You will hear melodies and feel rhythms that stem from his musical back ground. However these pieces stand alone, with or without form, for better or worse, as an insight to James' thought life and outward expression of internal musings. For more information on James Hickey visit www.heymus.com.

www.ingramcontent.com/pod-product-compliance
Lightning Source LLC
Chambersburg PA
CBHW052135010526
44113CB00036B/2273